MERCEDES-BENZ
LEGENDS

MERCEDES-BENZ
LEGENDS

David Sparrow & William Stobbs

OSPREY
AUTOMOTIVE

Published in Great Britain in 1993 by Osprey,
an imprint of Reed Consumer Books Limited,
Michelin House, 81 Fulham Road,
London SW3 6RB and Auckland, Melbourne,
Singapore and Toronto.
Reprinted spring 1997

ISBN 1 85532 676 0

Edited by Tony Holmes
Captions by John Tipler
Page design by Paul Kime
Printed in China

Acknowledgements

The authors are particularly indebted to the following individuals who helped during the
compilation of this volume; Max von Pein, Mercedes-Benz Unterturkheim, Deiter Ritter,
Dr H Niemann in Museum archives at Unterturkheim, Ernst D Beeh (President of the
Mercedes Vintage Club Germany), Roger King (President Mercedes Owners Club UK),
E K Hillgruber, Herman Layher (Museumsleitung, Sinsheim Museum), Luise Layher, Franz
Maag and his mechanic Charly Kaufengerer, Jurgen Kaufmann, Stefan Rohrig, Christopher
Renwick, Karl Sargent, Douglas Bryan, Sue Colby, Thomas Dangel and Jacob Maier
(German Auto Museum), Peter Scharwaechter, Karl Heike (designer AMG), Phillipe
Zucker, Chris Ridden, Tony Griscti, Wolfgang Inrester, J E White, Udo Lahm, Eberhard
Scholl, Claus D Brinkmann, Marcel van Schalk, Robin Gerretsen, Paul Ffolkes-Halbard,
Peterheinz Kern Dip Ing, Howard C Syndenhams and Hans Werner Aufrecht of AMG.

Front cover
*Dr Ferdinand Porsche developed the SSK for
racing. The Mercedes works team won
consistently with the car from 1929 to 1931,
notably the 1930 European Sports Car
Championship in 1930, Rudolf Caracciola at
the wheel. The 7068cc engine produced
225hp with supercharger.*

Back cover
*Mosselman Turbo Systems are based in the
Netherlands; they can fit just about any new
Mercedes with a turbo, aiming for high
torque at low revs.*

Half-title page
*Mercedes-Benz history takes on a sombre
note. With the advent of war in 1939,
production of cars was given over to support
the war effort, but by 1945 the factories had
been reduced to rubble by Allied bombing*

Title page
*Mercedes saloon cars in the mid 1930's
ranged from Pullman-Limousine types, based
on the 290, with sliding glass division and
cabriolet back, to simple fleet models based
on the 170V. The 260D came out in 1935,
the first Mercedes diesel passenger car, and
destined to become the mainstay of the
taxicab trade*

For a catalogue of all books published by Osprey Automotive
please write to:
**The Marketing Department, Reed Consumer Books,
1st Floor, Michelin House, 81 Fulham Road, London SW3 6RB**

Not an Edwardian traffic jam, but exhibits at the Mercedes-Benz museum at Unterturkheim, which has the enviable reputation of being the greatest one-marque museum in the world. This photograph actually shows two separate marques, Daimler and Benz cars from the early years of the century, for the two firms had yet to merge

Introduction

Mercedes-Benz engineering proves its quality and integrity day and night, on every autoroute in the world. In this volume we show its growth from vehicles made by two lonely pioneers, Benz and Daimler, to the present time, when there is a staff of 2500 at Sindelfingen in design alone, and a workforce of 231,000 producing annual sales of 60 billion DM.

Over the decades Daimler-Benz has faced challenging situations – suffering the Kaiser and Adolf Hitler, sidestepping inflation by printing Reichsmarks and enduring Gestapo infiltration during the war years.

Emerging from this chaos in 1948, having redesigned, not just rebuilt, the plant on modern lines, Daimler-Benz grew masterfully into a virtually impregnable world power.

Mercedes stock-market figures are currently almost off the charts, and the firm is one of the largest in the world

Their taxis, ambulances, trucks and stretched-limos rarely break, whether in polar ice or tropic heat, but should they do so 5900 service centres can fix them in 172 countries.

Wisdom and foresight on the part of the board of directors is probably the reason for their success. The brilliant opportunism in buying bankrupt companies, and turning them into gold mines, was the development route. Studebaker- Packard in 1964, Krupp, Henschel and Hanomag in 1966–67, Freightliner in 1981 and finally MTU and Dornier in 1985.

Mercedes-Benz have been producing perfection, but with wildly mounting costs. The future is at present balanced on a brink named 'cost effectiveness'.

Right
Wearing its hardtop, the 300SL is turned into a fine-looking coupe. As a touring car, it will return 24 mpg, giving a range of 350 miles. This is laudable, given the engine also has to power air conditioning, and there is a catalytic converter, power steering and an ABS braking system

Contents

Origins to World War 2

Karl Benz 1885–1926

Karl Benz designed and built the first machine driven by an internal combustion engine in 1885 at Mannheim, and Gottlieb Daimler built the second, in 1886, 60 kilometres away at Bad Cannstatt, and they were unaware of each other's existence.

Benz's ideas from the beginning were concerned with the car as an organic unit of chassis and engine. His first car was a tricycle with two driven rear wheels. This prototype still exists in the Deutsches Museum at Munich, to which it was presented by Karl Benz. There are many replicas about made by Daimler-Benz. This prototype already had features still used in today's vehicles; water cooling, electric ignition and a differential gear. It produced 75 bhp and was capable of achieving speeds of up to eight mph.

The first Benz four wheeler, the Victoria, was also the basis for the first van and bus, which were built in 1895. In 1898 pneumatic tyres were used on the Benz Comfortable, and in 1899 on the first Benz racing car. By this time the company had producted 603 cars.

In 1901 Benz sales declined because their designs appeared outdated when compared with the Mercedes made by Daimler. Benz replied with his parsifal, a two cylinder front-engined car with cardan drive. Then came a new four cylinder engine, and in 1903 a racing car with 60 bhp.

After many disagreements, Karl left the firm in 1903. When he returned in 1906 a glorious period of success with designer Hans Nibel was enjoyed by the company. The record of their achievements is as follow;

1907 – first, second and third in the Coppa Florio
first in the Florida 100 mile race

1908 – second and third in the French Grand Prix
second and fourth in the American Grand Prix

World speed records for Nibel in the 140-mph Blitzen Benz followed at Daytona.

Prince Henry of Prussia, meanwhile, was giving the right direction to the nobility of Europe by encouraging Benz to take part in the Austrian Alpine Trials.

Karl Benz began developing a two-stroke engine in 1877, transferring his attention to the four-stroke principal in 1885. His first car was ready a year later, rivalling the prototype of Gottlieb Daimler and Wilhelm Maybach. It was powered by a 924 cc engine, which propelled the vehicle along at a modest 9 mph, and was installed in a three-wheel frame with bench seating for riders

Above

The Benz Victoria models remained in production for some time, alongside the Mannheim factory's other cars like the Velo. Here is a detail of the Victoria's fuel tank. Speed was altered by a system of sliding drive belts over fast-running pulleys on a countershaft. This was preferred by many owners over the noisy gearboxes being developed at the time by other manufacturers

Left

Benz took an early lead in the fledgling motor industry, selling his vehicles in 1888 and employing some 50 personnel; the four-wheel Victoria was powered by a 3 hp 2.9-litre engine, featuring a vertical flywheel, float-fed carburettor and an ignition timing control which gave better performance and flexibility

The Kaiser, through his habit of being driven in a car powered by a racing engine, was also indirectly a supporter of Benz's work, and his Kaiser prizes for aero engines contributed significantly to the development of the internal combustion engine.

After the war Benz developed the diesel engine, which was first used to power tractors in 1922, followed by trucks in 1924. But at the time, despite good ideas, both companies were almost bankrupt, so Daimler and Benz amalgamated in 1926.

Gottleib Daimler 1834–1900

Gottlieb Daimler (1834–1900) served an apprenticeship to a gunsmith in his teenage years. Later he obtained a scholarship to Stuttgart Polytechnic, and at the age of 25, he met Wilhelm Maybach at the engineering works of the Bruderhaus Reutlingen, the company having taken him in as an orphan and educated him in their school. Gottlieb Daimler was fortunate to have this genius as a helper in the crucial years immediately prior to the turn of the century.

Eventually Maybach had to leave, first to design engines for Count Zeppelin, and later to found his own firm, and produce the legendary machines which bore his name.

Prior to his departure, he worked with Gottlieb to produce the world's first motorcycle in 1885, followed a year later by a carriage with an air-cooled single cylinder engine of 1.5 hp. In 1889 they produced a better car, with a tubular steel frame and wire wheels, called the Stahlradwagen.

When sent to the Paris World Fair, this vehicle laid the foundations of the French motor car industry as both Peugeot and Panhard-Levassor started production with this engine. Gottlieb became quite rich on the sale of engines, and later patents to France.

In 1890 the Daimler Motoren-Gesellschaft was founded, but by 1893 there were rows between the partners, so Daimler and Maybach left to start a workshop in the Hotel Hermann, a move which soon resulted in the production of the first atomizing carburettor.

In 1895 they returned to the firm, and by 1897 had produced the front-engined Phoenix, followed two years later by the first four cylinder engine of 28 hp. The powerplant was used by Emile Jellinek in the Nice Week races of that year, this legendary figure entering the event under the name of Monsieur Mercedes, which was his daughter's Christian name.

Jellinek was consular-general for the Austro-Hungarian Empire in Nice, and was already selling Daimler cars as an agent. Photographs of the time show him

The name Mercedes was first used in 1897 as a pseudonym by Emil Jellinek, a wealthy Daimler Phoenix owner, who entered the popular Nice motor sport events. It was actually the name of his eldest daughter, and he used it when obtaining the concession for the Maybach-designed Daimlers. In 1901, a team of these cars cleaned up in the Nice races, and the stage was set for the new Mercedes team to enter the Gordon Bennet races from 1903. This is a 1904 model, with fine honeycombed radiator grille, similar to the successful Mercedes Simplex Rennwagen raced by the great Camille Jenatzy

Above

Bird's eye view of the commanding driving position on the 1904 Mercedes. After Daimler died in 1900, Maybach went on to design the basis for this car; it had pressed steel chassis members instead of a wooden chassis, and a variable lift device as an extra means for controlling engine speed

Right

The 1904 Mercedes was powered by a 35 hp four cylinder engine with mechanically operated inlet valves. It was chain-driven, and the controls included two brake pedals, whilst mounted behind the bulkhead and on the footplate was a comprehensive array of gauges and the multiple sight feed lubricator

as a rather bizarre person, wearing a morning suit or a solar topee with pince-nez and riding breeches, but he was a keen driver and had good ideas on design. He insisted, for example, on a much lower centre of gravity, together with body streamlining.

The result of his recommendations was the Mercedes of 1901 – arguably the first modern motor car. Everyone had to have one. Jellinek then showed that in addition to style and sense in design, he also had a ruthless mind for business, demanding the right to be sole agent for the sale of Mercedes cars in most countries in Europe and America.

Note the gear selection gate, located by the driver's right hand side; in many ways the 1904 Mercedes was the pioneer of the motor car we know today. Being able to change gear in this way was a revolution compared with the problematic quadrant shift system. The entire vehicle was far more flexible, better handling and quieter than anything else around at the time

Mercedes 1901–1926

The 1901 Mercedes had a 35 bhp engine of 5.9 litres, a honeycomb radiator, gate change, mechanically operated inlet valves, Maybach's latest carburettor and a pressed steel frame. It was known as the 35PS.

The Mercedes Simplex models which followed were lighter and generally updated. The 60PS and 90PS racing cars, with their inlet over exhaust valves, were based on Simplex designs and achieved many successes including the 1903 Gordon Bennett race, the Ostend trials of 1904 and a world speed record attempt at Daytona in 1905.

Maybach left in 1907 and Paul Daimler assumed the role of chief engineer. He soon showed his ability by designing the 135PS racer, which won the 1908 French Grand Prix.

An epoch in the history of automobile design was Daimler's 115 bhp racing car, which was designed especially for the 1914 French Grand Prix. The vehicle duly took first, second and third! The car's powerplant was developed from the Daimler aero engine, which had won the Kaiser prize that same year.

One of the racers was subsequently despatched to the United States and won at Indianapolis. After World War 1 an old example was dusted off and raced to victory in both the Italian Grand Prix and the 1923 Targa Florio. This phenomenal engine was still winning races and trials in 1927.

Paul Daimler retired in 1922, and was succeeded by Ferdinand Porsche.

Mercedes-Benz 1926–1945

The amalgamation began with the new Stuttgart, a two litre, six cylinder 8/38PS, and the Mannheim, a 3 litre 12/55PS. Both designs were worthy, but conventional, the heavy SV monsters being equipped with three-speed boxes and wooden artillery wheels.

These vehicles were developed into the 260 Stuttgart and the 350 Mannheim, which, together with the Grosser, were the last cars to be built with the classic chassis, rigid axles and semi-elliptic springs, so beloved by today's collectors.

The model K, developed into the fabulous sports cars, started from the Mercedes 24/100/140PS, with shortened wheelbase and Roots supercharger – the 6.25 litre, 24/100/160PS was the fastest and most hallowed touring car of its time. This was the progenitor of the following models;

S	6.8 litre	26/120/180PS
SS	7 litre	27/140/200PS
SSK	7.1 litre	27/170/225PS
SSKL	7.1 litre	27/170/300PS

The Grosser Mercedes appeared in 1930 with a 7.7 litre engine developing either 150 bhp conventionally, or 200 bhp with a supercharger. These vehicles included every luxury within their sumptuous saloon bodies. Until 1937 it had that classic old chassis again, but from 1938 a tubular frame design with swing axles (which were to be a Mercedes trade mark for some time) was introduced, this machine benefitting from a power increase which pushed the available bhp to 230 and the top speed to 100 mph.

Further down the range, the 170 model was released in 1931. With a capacity of 1692 cc, the 170 had independent wheel suspension, a backbone chassis and built-in chassis lubrication, the latter usually being a feature of more expensive models. It was much appreciated as a solid, unbreakable and small workhorse. Hugely popular, more 170 models were built by Mercedes than any other car in their history. Their abundance in number is partly due to the fact that they were the only type built by the company immediately after the war while their factories were being reconstructed.

The 1930s was a period in which many collectors' classics were produced, but 1938 was an especially good year for Mercedes, with wins on the race track showing brilliant new technology. Backed by Hitler's enthusiastic support and financial aid, together with that new Germanic spirit which fascism brought with it, the company's grand prix machines were unbeatable.

It was also the year of the 500 and 540K coupes and cabriolets. The 500K convertible of 1935–36 was one of the most beautiful Mercedes ever built, and only five survive, two of which belong to Damler-Benz AG.

The SE cabriolets in particular, with the S-shaped metal hinge to the canvas roof, and the delicately shaped doors, which are thicker than most and made not to sag over the years (a disorder which most long cabriolet doors on other

The serpentine horn on the 1904 Mercedes, vital to warn unsuspecting pedestrians of the car's approach, since its original top speed was 80 mph – as if they wouldn't have been able to hear it coming! This fine machine belongs to Paul Ffolkes-Halbard, and it is regularly maintained and runs well today

makes find positively endemic), were in a class of their own. Production of the 500K cabriolet C (W 29) ran to 760 vehicles.

The 770K – the Grand Mercedes – of 1937 was an open tourer of the highest quality, with engineering and appointments never before seen to such a standard. Its eight cylinder engine initially produced 200 bhp with a supercharger, this figure being raised to 400 bhp in 1938.

Supercharged Mercedes

The Roots supercharger was designed by the Roots brothers Francis and Philander in the 1890s at Auburn, Indiana, to improve the family spinning wheel. A perfect answer to an engineering problem, it was widely used.

Ferdinand Porsche arrived at Mercedes in 1923, and using the Roots supercharged the old 10/40/65, increasing the power from 65 to 150 bhp. Then in 1926 Rudolf Caracciola won the German Grand Prix, and a further 21 races from 27 starts, in Porsche's 130/150.

Two versions of the SS were made for racing in 1931. The SSK appeared next. Porsche, restless and having moved on, was replaced by Nibel, Wenger and Nallinger, who made the SSK lighter by drilling out the chassis, which reduced the weight by 125 kilos. Renamed the SSKL (L for Leicht), the car was driven to victory by Caracciola in the 1931 Mille Miglia, the Avusrennen, the German Grand Prix and the Eifelrennen. Only seven SSKLs were made.

Superchargers were also used on street cars, including the Grosser Mercedes 770 between 1930 and 1939. Next, the 380/380Ks appeared with independent suspension and a supercharger.

The 500Ks of 1934 were full of style, but there is a formidable difference between the 500K and today's engine management miracles. The 500K had a mixture control on the steering wheel for example, which needed the right setting.

This 500 was superseded by the 540/540K in 1936, which had a 180 bhp blown engine – good for 106 mph. – and made it the fastest European car of 1936.

Although Mercedes is a well-known name today, the corporate identity and nomenclature was confusing at the time of its inception. Daimler himself was dead, Maybach designed the car, so Jellinek, Austrian Consul-General in Nice from 1900, provided the identity through his racing. He was elected to the board in 1901. Such was the reputation of the Mercedes that it was sought by customers such as King Leopold of Belgium

Above

At a time when Germany had no fewer than 86 different motor manufacturers producing 144 different models, Mercedes and Benz cars did well to win races. But times were hard in the austere post-war years, and because of swinging luxury tax and a glut of foreign imports, it made sense to consolidate. Thus Benz and Cie and Daimler Motoren Gesellschaft merged in June 1926. Here are three vehicles from that period in the museum at Unterturkheim

Left

The 600K of 1926 was based on the supercharged six litre six-cylinder car designed by Dr Porsche and first seen in 1922. This was developed into the K-model by shortening the wheelbase, enlarging the engine to 6.25 litres, and at 110 hp without supercharger or 160 hp with blower, it was the fastest touring car in the world. Its reputation ensured sustained demand for the company's high-performance tourers during the late 1920s and early 1930s. A number were bodied by the leading coachbuilders of the time like Saoutchik, Castagna and Farina

A range of worthy, well made saloons, which earned the company its bread and butter, started to appear in the early 1930s. The Type 290 of 1933 began with a squarish windscreen profile, later developing a more sporting appearance. Contemporary was the Junkers Ju 52 airliner, perched ominously overhead at the Sinsheim Museum

Above

Magnificent scenery, magnificent car: one of the great show-stoppers, a 540K Special Roadster getting an airing out in the mountains. Based on the 280 chassis, this was one of a number of extravagant designs done in the early 1930s, with long, elegant flowing wings and running-boards, curvaceous rear wheelarches and a sloping flat deck behind

Right

Sibling of the bigger-engined SS, short-chassis SSK and lightweight SSKL, this is a 1926 S-type (S for Sport), powered by a 6.8-litre light-alloy engine. These models were long, low four seaters sold in the UK as 36/220s. The S-type proved to be less clumsy than it looked thanks to refined steering geometry and excellent handling characteristics

Above

No mistaking the purpose of the SSK; the 'SS' stands for Super Sport, the 'K' stands for kurtz, or short, and the SSK is a short-chassis version of the 27/140/200 SS sports tourer, which used semi-elliptic leaf-springs on a beam axle at the front and a live axle and leaf-springs at the rear. Legendary works driver Rudolf Caracciola brought one of these cars into third place in the hugely demanding Monaco Grand Prix of 1930

Left

Although cars like this SSK of 1929 were not built as racing cars, they were frequently pressed into service as such, by stripping off the mudguards and superfluous items like headlights. They were able to prevail over purpose-built racing machinery, winning events like the Ulster TT in 1929, the Irish Grand Prix in 1930, the German Grand Prix in 1931 and perhaps more remarkably, the Mille Miglia in the same year

Above

Taken to its furthest extent, the SSKL ('L' is for licht, or lightened) had its chassis drilled with large holes, and used a massive 'elephant' supercharger to take its power output up to 300 bhp. Driving an SSKL, Caracciola took the 1931 figure-eight Mille Miglia single handed, and as a gauge of the car's capabilities, he averaged 95.8 mph over the 129-mile stretch from Brescia to Bologna. It could easily do 130 mph

Left

An SSK on familiar territory at the Salzburgring; when Dr Porsche and the Mercedez-Benz board elected to go for the greater prestige of sports car racing because the Grand Prix category was in the doldrums, the SSK was evolved. By 1928, Porsche had departed, and his place was taken by Hans Nibel, who had designed the Blitzen Benz. With increased kompressor, or supercharger pressure, the SSK could deliver 250 bhp. Just 33 SSKs were commissioned for production

Above

Two kinds of touring here, as a sporting SSK follows a more stately model K on the Salzburgring. The 6.2-litre K was the natural successor to the 6-litre 24/100/140. Note the right hand drive steering position, which was traditional in top class cars in Europe right up to World War 2

Above right

Fine shot of an S-type, a left-hooker this time, with all weather equipment on board. The low-line sporting chassis is powered by a 6.8-litre engine with a four-speed gearbox. The drivetrain included a torque tube enclosing the propshaft, and spiral bevel-gear differential

Right

Given the chance, you could easily spend all day tinkering with your Mercedes. Note the massive semi-elliptic leaf springs protruding from the front of the car, as well as the horn, headlights and badge-bar. There are two Mercedes three-cornered stars on the radiator surround, which identify this as an S-type, as well as the one on the actual radiator cap. The SS, SSK and SSKL have just one central star on the radiator

Detailing of the S-type's impressive exhaust manifolding, which is one of the car's chief visual characteristics. The six exhaust ports emerge individually, and are quickly siamesed to leave the engine compartment as three huge pipes which disappear under the running board. On models without the running board the system can be seen more readily

Above

Spectacular scenery for the Vintage Mercedes Club on tour in the Austrian Lakes in 1992, with a pair of S-series cars and a very rare late 1930s beetle-backed, rear-engined 130 saloon viewed almost through the 'gunsight' of the three-cornered star of the Mercedes badge

Left

Lakeside scene with beach hut features a standard model S-series tourer from 1927. Like the K-type, chassis were sold to many of the eminent carrozzerie of the period, like Zietz of Geneva, Van den Plas of Brussels, Freestone and Webb of London, and Erdmann and Rossi of Germany, who built one for Caracciola himself. Mercedes-Benz built their own bodies as well, and the theme was always fairly similar

Above

Left-hand drive dashboard of a Stuttgart 10/50, showing 160 kmph speedometer, clock and switchgear. The white knob at the top is for opening the windscreen for ventilation, and the steering wheel has a horn-ring. Two new models appeared in 1926. These were a pair of heavy, side-valve sixes, one a 2.6-litre known as the Stuttgart, and the other a 3.1-litre model which was the Mannheim, and so-called because that was where they were built

Right

Photographed outside the ruined Krupp armament factory at Essen is a 1930 Mannheim 350 (3.5-litres) Limousine designed by Dr Porsche. A narrow chrome strip running over the bonnet betrays creeping American influence; note the running boards and foot-plates

Above

Spare wheel on this 540K is typically white-walled in the best ostentatious tradition; when these cars were shipped to the USA in the late 1930s, they were shod with wooden tyres for transit purposes, in a bid to conserve rubber in Germany

Left

Louvred left-hand portion of the bonnet raised on a gaudy 500K, the overblown sports tourer which took the place of the SS. These vulgar beasts were based on the 280 chassis, and weighed in at around 5500 lbs. They were powered by eight-cylinder pushrod engines. In kompressor form, the 540K was capable of 105 mph, with a 0–60 mph time of 14 seconds. Power output was 180 bhp, and 115 bhp without supercharger

Above

Another version of the 540K, showing the cutaway treatment of the leading edge of the front wings. There is generally a more sporting feel to this car, and it has a central spotlight and 'rally' style lights by the cockpit. The split front bumper treatment indicates that this is an early model

Right

A 5.4-litre 540K cabriolet featuring bulbous front wings; this model could be ordered with a variety of body-styles, from saloon and open tourer to fixed head coupe and sports roadster. You could specify three types of cabriolet depending on whether you wanted a two- or four-seater, and whether you wanted rear three-quarter windows or not. Sports models had spare wheels located in the tail, while the tourers had a spare mounted in each of the front wings

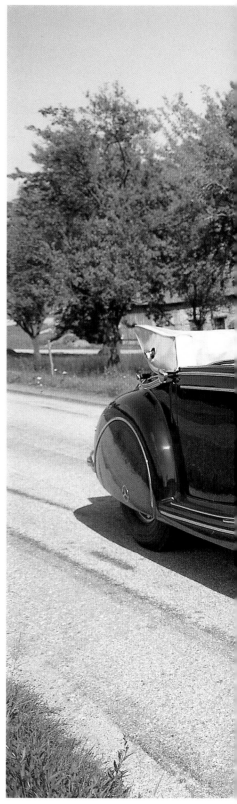

Above

Hinge detailing on a 1937 320 cabriolet. The cabriolets and roadsters were built on a shortened 320 chassis, and are favoured by collectors. The chassis was a box-frame design, with all independent suspension, and 320 implies a 3.2-litre straight-six side-valve engine

Right

Direct access to the radiator is obtained by removing the silver star. This is a special bodied four-door 500K Streamliner, circa 1936; split windscreens like this are rare in Mercedes styling

Above

The 78 bhp 320 was one of a range of three new models introduced by Mercedes in 1937; the others were the 230 and 290 series cars, and the 320 cabriolets were particularly notable because of the curving lines of the wings and general body shape, which pre-figured the contours of the post-war 170, 220 and 300 cabriolets

Right

Overhead view of the 320 cabriolet, showing the cream leather upholstered four-seater layout, contrasting with the vast black folded hood. Note the four-spoke steering wheel and twin spare wheels. There was a four-speed gearbox, and top speed was a leisurely 126 kmph

The 320 cabriolet, resplendent in bright scarlet coachwork and matching disc wheels, posed in front of distincly Modernist architecture of the 1930s avant garde Europe. Car and building would probably have been roughly contemporary

Above

A glimpse of the sumptuous interior of the 540K, pictured on tour in the Austrian lakes. Note the windscreen wiper mounting on top of the screen. Another feature of this model is the large knock-off hubcap and 17-inch wire-spoked wheel

Left

Continuing the supercharged line, the 540K was one of the kompressor models produced from 1936 to 1939. It was endowed with striking looks and 180 bhp from its 5.4-litre straight-eight engine. As can be seen from the huge hood overhanging the tail, this is a cabriolet version, with spares mounted on the side rather than on the tail, which was more common, although a matter of personal preference. The 540K had exposed exhaust pipes on its right-hand side

An S-series open tourer taking part in the Vintage Mercedes Club rally in Austria in 1992. These cars had wire wheels with small knock-off hubs, and this car has tapered doors and a period trunk fixed to the rear

Above

Our driver is dreaming of those halcyon days when Mercedes-Benz ruled the Grand Prix circuits, perhaps. This is a factory-bodied SS cabriolet, a touring car as well as a snoozing car, evidently. A mere 107 SS cars was produced betwen 1927 and 1935

Left

Two spares on the tail instead of either side. The wheel fastening arrangement and rear-end styling indicate that this is a 380 Cabriolet A, made during 1933/34, and undoubtedly one of the most attractive of the straight-eight cars. This model was the replacement for the S-series, and consequently there was more attention paid to creature comforts. It is related to the 500 and 540K, but has a shorter chassis and lacks the external exhaust pipes

A 540K cabriolet, seen at the Salzburgring. This handsome cab is a B or C model, implying that it has four seats; correct identification is only possible with the hood up. The small lip on the running board above the jacking point suggests that this is a factory body

Above

A 500K with a different set of clothes; this is a four-door saloon bodied 'Streamliner', one of a rare series of cars built on the 500K platform and using appropriate running gear like the 17-inch wire wheels and knock-off hub caps

Left

This series of streamlined cars followed on from the Autobahn-Kurier, a coupe with a steeply curved rear end and spats covering the rear wheels, and the closest a Mercedes-Benz got to the fabulous late 1930s Grand Routier style. The saloon is exceedingly rare, since only two exist

Overleaf

Supremely elegant for a Mercedes 500K, the Streamliner's doors are hinged on a central pillar, so that the fronts are 'suicide' doors and the rears open conventionally. Whereas the roadster models have short cockpits and hence the engines and radiators are set further back behind the front wheels, the stylistic treatment of this car brings the running gear right up between them

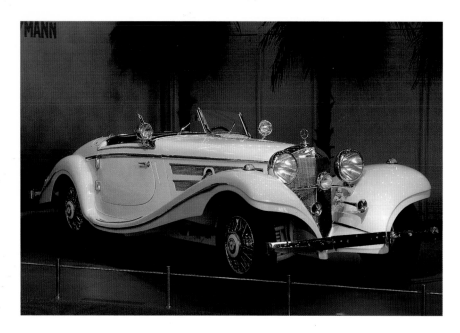

Above

Most blatantly exotic of the 540Ks, this is the Special Coupe with extravaganty cutaway front wings. Other distinguishing features are the louvred bonnet, stove-pipe exhausts, split windscreen with spotlamps mounted close by, and a central spotlight flanked by air-horns. A coachline follows the swooping curvature of the wings and runningboard

Right

Over the top? Only very. The 540K Special Coupe was the one to get noticed in. In fact the car probably got more attention than the occupants. It could be ordered with extra fuel tanks on the running boards, although it has been suggested that these could be used to contain refreshments of a different kind

Above

It's the turn of the 320 Cabriolet to get an airing on the Salzburgring. Its six-cylinder 3.2-litre engine develops 78 bhp at 4000 rpm, pushing it to a top speed of 126 kmph. Armco and adverts somehow don't gel with the refined image of 1930s motoring

Left

Enjoying their annual beano in Austria, members of the Vintage Mercedes Club take a trip round the Salzburgring circuit in a 540K Cabriolet. These kompressor cars were admittedly powerful, developing 180 bhp at 3400 rpm which resulted in a maximum speed of 170 kmph, but they actually had less horsepower than the S-series cars of ten years earlier

Above
There are two advantages in having six wheels on your wagon. Firstly the weight of any load carried is spread over two axles, and secondly the vehicle has better traction in hostile terrain. Ideal for the military really. This machine is in the museum at Sinsheim

Left
A blast through the deserted pine forests, top down, straight-sixes and eights wailing; what could be better? A 320 Cabriolet and 540K on full song provide the entertainment

Overleaf
So clean you could eat your dinner off it; there are no lengths some enthusiasts will not go to in the quest for concours condition judging by this inlet manifolding detail

Mercedes-Benz 1945–1990

The factories at Unterturkheim, Sindelfingen and Gaggenau had been largely destroyed by 1945, but they were rebuilt with future forms of car production in mind.

Car manufacturing started again in 1946 with the revised 170 model of the late 1930s. The new 170, with its lead-bronze bearings for mains and big ends, was capable of achieving up to 75 mph on the autobahn.

By 1950 Mercedes was producing 800 of these cars a week, utilizing a workforce of 3200. Such was Germany's recovery however, that people were eager for greater power, speed and luxury. At the 1951 Frankfurt show, Mercedes presented the Fritz Nallinger and Rudolf Uhlenhaut designed 220, 300 and 300S, which had all the things German customers demanded.

The 220, based on a cruciform chassis with coil and wishbones, was powered by a 2.2 litre six of 80 bhp, but sadly the body still had pre-war styling. The 300 and 300S were a major advance in engineering; all three cars had four-speed manual boxes, and column mounted levers.

When the ban on international racing was lifted in 1951, Rudolf Uhlehhaut took over Neubauer's old job, and sent a team of the old three litre W163s to the Argentine Grand Prix, where they finished second and third behind a Ferrari.

It was the 300SL which was the basis for a comeback to racing in 1952, the car winning four out of six events, as well as Le Mans and the Mexican Pan Americana. The body of the gullwing was outstanding, but the 220 looked rather plain.

Meanwhile the old 170 was replaced by the 180, which still had a side valve engine of 52 bhp. This veteran model was soon replaced by the 220a, which was powered by a six cylinder overhead camshaft engine.

By 1955 the Daimler-Benz range consisted of the 220a six, the 300, with various bodies, and the 190SL and 300SL sports cars, together with the extremely popular Unimog four-wheel drive truck-cum tractor.

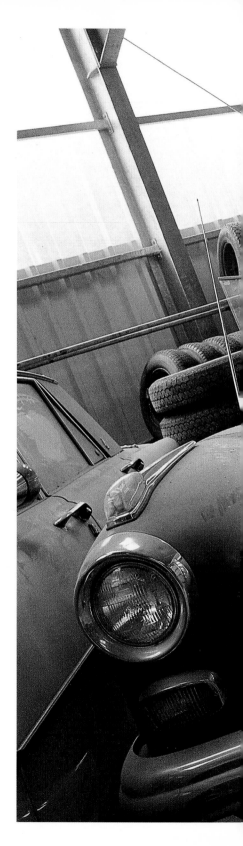

A 220 awaits some tender loving care at the Sinsheim museum. This series was produced from 1951 to 1960, and was the first Mercedes to have the headlights incorporated into the front wings. Driving lights were usually round, but this car's are small rectangular jobs. Power was provided by a 2.2-litre six-cylinder engine, which had an iron block and aluminium single overhead camshaft head. This engine survived largely unchanged until 1973

The Race Track

Daimler-Benz then returned to the track with the W196, a new unblown 2.5 litre straight-eight, which had one-piece forged cylinder bores and combustion chambers. The engine was two back-to-back fours, with a central gear train for the overhead camshafts and a central power take-off, which eliminated torsional vibrations in the crankshaft, running in ten roller bearings and carrying forged con-rods in ball races. A geared-down subshaft transferred the drive to the clutch and trans-axle five-speed gearbox.

The new engineering element which made its debut in this car (and researched by Dr Ing H Scherenberg) was the use of two large valves per cylinder at an angle of 90 degrees. These were positively opened and closed by a desmodromic system, capable of 9000 rpm. The engine also benefitted from Bosch direct fuel injection.

Suspension was by swing axle, plus Watts linkage and torsion bars, and braking by huge inboard drums operated by special shafts, instead of discs. The chassis was by small diameter tubes, similar to the Maserati bird cage concept.

The W196 proved itself by the end of the year and Fangio won his second world title. For 1955 Mercedes had another racing car, the W196S – or 300SLR – which also featured a staight eight and desmodromics. It was with this version that Fangio and Moss almost dead heated at the Eifelrennen, and again at the Belgian Grand Prix.

The 1955 disaster at Le Mans actually occured in one of these machines, Frenchman Pierre Levegh cannoning off an Austin Healey into the crowd. As a result of this horrific accident the French and German Grand Prixs were immediately cancelled. Mercedes, however, were first and second in the following three events, and finished the year off with a victory in the Targa Florio. The factory then withdrew from racing.

This 300Sc Cabriolet used an efficient 3-litre Bosch fuel-injected straight-six engine, and was very much the luxury class of the Mercedes-Benz range. The 300Sc could be ordered with four doors, although this model has just the two. It was built on a tubular steel chassis, and featured all-independent suspension, with a single-pivot swing-axle at the rear. Power output was 175 bhp at 5400 rpm, top speed was 112 mph, and fuel consumption about 14 mpg. Automatic transmission was optional

Road Cars

The mid 1950s saw new technology like the revolutionary Bosch fuel injection system introduced throughout the range, vehicles like the 300SLR, 300 saloon and the 220SE immediately feeling the performance benefits of this new engineering. The 220 also had a new bodyshell, with vertically designed headlights and a tail with vestigial fins.

The 230SL, presented at the 1963 Geneva Show, had a concave roof line, improved suspension and fuel injection, which gave the car a 120 mph top speed. This model was followed by the 250 and 280SLs, none of which were out and out sports car like the 300SL.

In 1963 came the grand 600s, which were aimed squarely at the prestige market. The new 6.3 litre V8 was superbly engineered, and also powered a central hydraulic system which controlled more or less everything.

New Models 1965–1970

The 200 series retained the fintail, but the later 250/280/300 models with vertical headlights had lower bodies. The swinging rear axles were finally replaced, after 30 years, with a semi-trailing layout.

As an interesting sidelight, following consumer protection crusader Ralph Nader's blitz on car safety in the mid 1960s, many features which Mercedes had used for years in their cars were listed as newly introduced in 1968 just to reassure the American market.

The Uhlenhaut SL roadsters and SLC coupes were replaced in 1971 by the 350SL and SLC, the latter being powered by V8 engines in an effort to ward off competition from BMW. In 1973 the power was further increased for the 450SLCs, whilst at the top of the range the 450SEL with a 6.9 litre engine (capable of 140 mph) was quietly phased in.

Construction of the 1952 300S, pictured here, was very similar to the 220 and 170-series, using a tubular chassis but metal body frame rather than wood. Production of the series lasted from 1951 to 1962, and the cars tended to be owned by wealthy sporting enthusiasts. The hood was naturally very well constructed, and was generously lined with horsehair

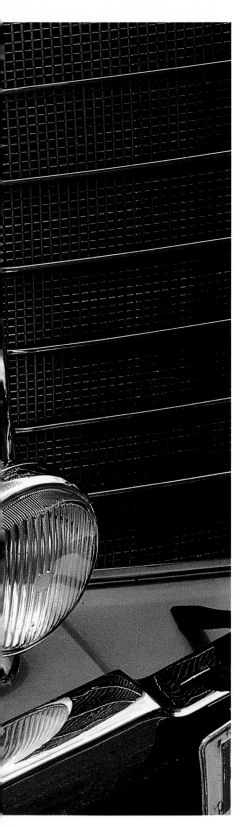

Above

Neat understated lettering and logo on the bootlid of the 300S. There was a four-speed gearbox with column shift, and a servo controlled the rear suspension settings if a heavy load was being carried

Left

All fittings are superbly integrated into the facade of the 300S. This model was very expensive, easily matching Rolls-Royce territory, and all the best materials and manufacturing techniques were used in its construction. Inside, there was a degree of opulence and the occupants were cosseted with wooden veneer dashboard and trim, leather upholstery, and a push-button wireless

The 300S marked a post-war return to the real Mercedes-Benz, being elegant and well proportioned, yet having real presence with the tall radiator grille. As a consequence, the S and Sc have become extremely desirable on the collectors' market, reaching the heady realms of 300SL values

CIII

A laboratory on wheels, the first CIII was to be an indicator of future trends in design. The project was controlled by Dr Hans Liepold, and the first production vehicle to benefit from it was the S series saloon, which featured the CIII's front suspension layout when it was released in 1972.

Rudolf Uhlenhaut was also involved with the CIII, and in 1970 he test drove the car. Exhibited in Geneva, the vehicle drew blank cheques from many cognoscenti but Mercedes were disinterested.

Daimler-Benz have had an unnatural affection for diesels but proved their sagacity with remarkable world records. Maximum revs of 4200 to 4700 rpm produced 190 bhp and speeds of 160 mph on the Nardo circuit, creating several new records.

The research director, however, thought that speeds in excess of 185 mph should have been possible, so in 1977 the styling department produced drawings for a new vehicle, the CIII–III. Professor Werner Breitschwert was in charge this time. The new body produced even less drag than the previous CIII, and on 30 April 1978 the CIII–III set no less than nine sustained speed world records.

CIII–IV

The next instalment in the CIII saga was the petrol-engined CIII–IV, which was designed to beat the Can-Am Porsche circuit record of the time.

A standard V8 as used in the S series SLC models was selected, and duly bored out to 4.8 litres. A triple plate clutch was needed to harness the 500 bhp produced by the modified powerplant. Lateral acceleration, which had been 0.2g on the CIII–III, rose to 0.4g. The effect of the track's banking would press the car against the ground to raise wheel loading to 3500 lbs, and this resulted in problems for the vehicle's tyre manufacturer, Michelin, who could not guarantee more than 30 minutes at 250 mph. A tyre blow out at 250 mph with a lateral acceleration of 0.4g would have been catastrophic.

200 mph in a diesel? True enough. This 235 bhp CIII record breaker lives in the Mercedes museum at Unterturkheim. It is a close relative of the pair of Wankel rotary-engined prototypes, with gull-wing doors, built by the factory in 1969 and 1970 to assess the possibilities of going into production with a real supercar. Although performance of the second four-rotor version was close to the diesel's, at 190 mph and 350 bhp, the CIII project was not taken further

Above

The fabulous W196 300SLR (or W196/110) of 1954/55. Related to the all-conquering Grand Prix car driven by Fangio and Moss, this was the machine driven by Moss and Jenkinson to win the Mille Miglia in 1955. The intention had always been to raise its 3-litre engine's power output from the original 256 bhp to some 400 bhp with the help of four-wheel-drive. However, the fatal accident at Le Mans, in which Pierre Levegh crashed his 300SLR into the crowded grandstand, put an end to Mercedes' works racing involvement for some 30 years

Left

There's a limit to how many exhibits you can take in one go at these places. When it all gets too much, the Mercedes museum provides an airy high-tech setting for recharging the human batteries

The dignitaries' special: a short-wheelbase 600 limousine, normally chauffeur driven, with 6.3-litre fuel-injected V8 engine, had the most lavish specification imaginable. It included air suspension and adjustable dampers, two heater and air conditioning systems, hydraulic door and boot opening, plus a drinks cabinet; the list is seemingly endless

When completed the CIII–IV was another stunning beauty, its body crafted in polished aluminium and bedecked with sophisticated assymetrical spoilers. Dr Hans Liebold performed the test runs, which culminated in a new world record of 250.91 mph.

Mercedes S Class 1972/79/85

Launched in 1972 at the Paris Show, the Mercedes S class cars were to be impeccable, the best in the world in every respect, and with new models appearing every seven years in order to be technically innovative at all times, these machines proved hard to fault.

The first engine was the M116, a 3.5 litre V8, with 200 bhp, which also pioneered the Robert Bosch electronic engine management system. There was also the M110 engine with an aluminium alloy cylinder head, classical hemispheres, and a crank with 12 counter weights, plus vibration damper. Finally, the automatic transmission now used a torque converter, instead of a fluid flywheel, mainly to satisfy the Americans.

The body was basically the same, except it had a few mild aerodynamic features such as a more sloping windscreen, lowered radiator grill and smoother outline, but weight had increased considerably due to the extra safety features – stronger safety cell, improved roll-over stiffness, and side impact resistance. Increased engine power compensated for all this.

Steady downsizing by other manufacturers of various models throughout the 1970s was not copied by Mercedes, and S class ran to its full capacity of 63,000 units annually, with minimal changes.

Front suspension by double wishbones and coils, rear by semi-trailing arms, plus anti-squat to resist weight transfer on hard acceleration, made a huge difference when compared to the former swing axle models.

Friedrich von Winsen was chief engineer for the new1979 S class and his brief was positive – S class cars cover twice the mileage, and with a larger number of passengers, than all other cars, therefore no downsizing. When the new model appeared it had a lighter, low drag body, new V8 engine and a new four-speed automatic transmission which had cost somewhere in the region of three million pounds per annum in research and development, and had included changing the tracks for the indispensable robots.

Dynamically, both the 380 and 500 had the ability to put more miles into the day, and with the hydro-pneumatic suspension, all in perfect tranquility.

The 1985 S class changed the classical shape ever so slightly – new skirts front and rear, lower panels in a different material and wider tyres (205/65). The new engines had EXL (microprocessor-controlled regulating functions) to obtain optimal use of fuel which produced the lowest pollutants. Finally, the front axle was now designed so that even a flat tyre would not deflect the steering.

SL and SLC Sports Cars 1945–1990

The tradition of the two-door sports coupe began with the Gullwing 300SL of the 1950s. Today's model has an automatic ADS (adaptive damping system) which is not only sensitive to changes in the road surface, but also to your driving flaws – a roll bar rises automatically when electronic sensors detect anything untoward in your driving.

The electro-hydraulically operated soft top, operated by a single button, and the advanced seats with a memory, show how the designers have been working to refine the breed. However, even with all these creature comforts Mercedes made sure that the power output of the 300SL still placed the machine ahead of its rivals.

Between the classic 300SL and the current cars there have been several SLs and SLCs with real quality, almost all of which were designed by Rudolph Uhlenhaut, who had also been responsible for many pre- and post-war racing cars.

He designed the 230SL, which started a whole family of SLs and SLCs that are today probably the most desirable of all Mercedes to own and drive. These were followed in 1967 by the 250, and later the 280, which had disc brakes all round and generally benefitted from reduced maintenance costs.

The 350SL and 450SLCs continued the classic sporting lines, the finesse in design being equally matched by engine horsepower. The 450 for example produced 225 bhp and was capable of cruising at 135 mph. The powerplant for the 500SL of 1977 was good for a steady 240 bhp at 5000rpm, whilst the top of the range 500SEC of 1981 was made mainly for customers in the Arabian states.

When Mercedes-Benz re-entered the motor sporting arena in 1952, the chosen weapon was the 300SL. A highly-tuned version of the 3-litre engine powered the 300s, and was canted over at an extraordinary 45-degree angle. Installed in a sophisticated multi-tubular spaceframe chassis, the car was raced under the direction of engineer Rudi Uhlenhaut and manager Alfred Neubauer. It was an instant success, with wins at Le Mans and the Carrera Panamericana, as well as the sports car Grands Prix of Switzerland and Germany

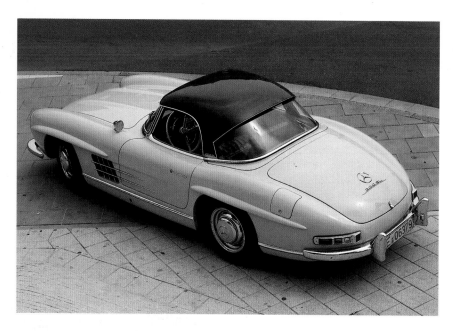

Above

A 300SL (SL is for Super Light) coupe-roadster has its hard-top attached, and the hood is hidden away. Conventional doors replace the gullwings, and one of the clever idiosyncrasies of these beautiful long, low, cars is the door handles, which spring out at the touch, to be used lever fashion to open the door. The 300SL coupe-roadster model was in production from 1957 to 1963

Right

The first of the 300SL coupes had upward-opening gullwing doors, providing greater rigidity, and the streamlined bodies were an instant hit. The one drawback was that the side windows did not wind down, although they could be removed. 300SLs used the same spaceframe chassis construction as the racing versions, and were available from 1954. Unusually, the coupe is more valuable than the sports model, as the reverse is usually true; however, in this case it is the gullwing coupe which has the racing pedigree

Although this gullwing coupe has regular painted hub caps, knock-off competition lock-nuts could be specified. Since the spare wheel occupied most of the boot space, fitted leather suitcases were popular options. For the road-going versions, 215 bhp was available from the 3-litre straight-six, with a maximum of 145 mph and acceleration to match

Above

This 190SL, with the National Motor Museum at Beaulieu as a background, has aquired an additional badge and a pair of driving lamps. Overriders were options not fitted to this car. It was launched at the Geneva Show in 1954, and subsequently there were three versions; roadster, closed coupe and detachable hardtop coupe. Production ended in 1963, by which time 26,000 units had been made

Left

Little sister of the 300SL, the 190SL has the same good looks, but less aggressive posture. It was intended to sell to enthusiasts, principally in the USA, who wanted something a bit more affordable than the 300SL. There was a floorpan chassis rather than a spaceframe, and it was powered by a dry-sump, four-cylinder 1897 cc unit, fed by twin Solex carbs, and developing 105 bhp at 5700 rpm, which gave a top speed of 110 mph

Above
Stylists gave the 190SL strakes over the wheelarches redolent of the 300SL, although the smaller-engined car has clearly defined rear wings. Inside there are no sporting pretentions, and it comes over as a well-appointed long distance touring machine

Right
The 190SL had a single power-bulge on its bonnet rather than the two of the six-cylinder model, and this car has the optional overriders. It was a slightly taller car than the 300SL, and despite modest performance, handling, roadholding and braking were its strongpoints

Above

The 300d was known as a hardtop limousine, and was introduced in 1957 with automatic transmission and an uprated 160 bhp 3-litre engine. Whilst the 300d majored on luxury, its sister car, the 300S tourer, was the most expensive poduction car in Germany in the late 1950s

Right

There was a fashion for hard-tops in the 1950s, and the rigid body of the 300d allowed the central B-pillar to be dispensed with, and once the windows were wound down and the rear side windows removed, it gave an airy pillarless configuration similar to the big American sedans. Inside was great luxury, with upholstery in leather, velvet or cord

Above
Short- and long-chassis 600 Pullman Limousines were built on a special production line because there were so many extra features and options to be incorporated. In its most prolific year, 1965, only 345 units were made, and by 1974 production had fallen to just 25 vehicles. By the time production ended in 1981, 2677 type-600s had been built

Above right
Powered by a new 6332 cc fuel-injected V8, the 600 has a pressurised air suspension system which is self-adjusting, allowing for fluctuations in ride height and firmness. This required an engine driven compressor, as did the power steering and dual-circuit braking system with its twin sets of front calipers. It was a highly sophisticated machine indeed

Right
The Grosser versions of the 600 came with either four or six doors on a long-wheelbase chassis. As Europe became afflicted by successive oil crises, financial and environmental issues, demand for the cars waned, with orders coming mostly from the US and the Middle East

Above

One good thing about Mercedes cars is that the body shapes don't alter rapidly. This 220SEb cabriolet is a 1965 car, but it has basically the same body as the 1972 280SE. Rear seats were larger in the 220SEb than its predecessor from the 1950s, and by 1965, it had gained fuel injection and disc brakes, and the 2195 cc straight-six was good for 120 bhp and 107 mph

Right

The three versions of the handsome SL roadster, the 230, 250 and 280, are simply developments of engine capacity, and all share the same body styling. Four-speed automatic gearboxes are more common than the optional four- or five-speed manual boxes. Introduced in 1968, the 280SL catered for US federal emission regulations, and the capacity increase provided greater torque to compensate for this

Above

The 280SL series had removable hard tops, dubbed the 'pagoda roof', and once removed, the hood could be easily erected. Mercedes afficionados regard the 230SL as the nicest of the range because it has firmer, more sporting handling characteristics, and is lighter and lacks the anti-smog equipment of the later models

Right

Further differences between the SLs included the four-wheel disc brake systems of the two larger capacity models, the 230SL having front discs only; the 250SL had a larger fuel tank, the 280SL a more luxurious interior and a power steering option

Above
The 350SL superseded the 250SL in 1970, and it was equipped with the 3.5-litre
V8 of the 280SE coupe. This advanced unit used electronic fuel injection and
transistorized ignition, and produced 200 bhp, enabling a top speed of 127 mph.
The 450SL of 1972 was heavier and laden with a catalytic converter, and eventually
incorporated an auxilliary underbonnet cooling device because of fuel vapourisation
problems

Left
The 230SL was introduced in 1963. Its 2306 cc straight-six could power it to 124
mph, although the swing axle rear suspension, descended from the 300SL, was the
Achilles' heel; it permitted undesirable camber changes to take place, which under
heavy braking caused traction problems. It called for circumspect driving technique
and careful use of the accelerator

Above
First of the S-class saloons, the 280E ran with a six-cylinder engine, but the range included 2-litre four-cylinders and diesel engines. They were essentially well-made, reliable and competent workhorses

Left
As had become traditional with Mercedes sports cars, the hardtop of the 350SL was removable, with the hood folded behing the rear seat squab. Again, there is a timeless quality about this series, because the 380SL and 500SL of 1980 have identical panelling, just bigger but lighter engines. Production ceased in 1986

Current Models

S Class

As every S class appears it makes the previous one obsolete. This has been the case every seven years since 1972. The classical shape changes only slightly each time, as though a basic body shell was being honed towards some ultimate concept. The first S class was a considerable leap forward for Mercedes in technological terms as it pioneered the use of both Bosch electronic management and Bosch Jetronic fuel injection, which together changed the whole concept of performance motoring.

The 1979 S benefitted from a new computer designed body shape, which was considerably lighter and created less drag. Under the skin the car was powered by a new V8 engine, which was geared through an improved four-speed automatic box.

These modifications resulted in better fuel efficiency and improved performance. Again in 1985 came more subtle refinements, but the current S is on a different plateau altogether.

1991 S Class Engines

The high point of the new S class powerplant is a more comprehensive engine management system. Networks of electronic control devices perform together as a databus system, designated CAN (controller area network). Control modules communicate with one another, via a joint data channel, to encompass additional functions not previously possible.

These network control units operate as a team, so several things happen simultaneously. For example, rapid heating of the catalytic converter after cold starting the engine takes place automatically, while for the acceleration skid management, there is friction torque control from the engine, ensuring handling stability.

Also, there is independent electronic monitoring of all control devices. Electronics are all housed in a box screened against thermal or electromagnetic disturbances situated in the boot.

Mercedes estate cars have a well justified reputation for unbustable build quality, and although efficient enough, they are somewhat dull to drive. 200TE, 230TE, and TD are the basic models, and there is a 24-valve TE capable of 147 mph

Above

The short-wheelbase 300 G-Wagen (G is for Gelandewagen) is massively built and trespassing on traditional Land Rover and Range Rover territory, especially in the case of the long-wheelbase version. Robust and rugged, they are highly efficient off-roaders, yet not so spartan that they are unfamiliar in the city

Right

Off-roading does not require great resources of speed, but low-down torque helps, and the 3-litre diesel unit pictured here does a very good job for the G-Wagen. There is versatile cargo space, and the specification, which includes permanent four-wheel drive and anti-lock brakes, was originally evolved in collaboration with Steyr-Daimler-Puch

A diagnostic system designed to analyse the CAN bus is used when the vehicle is serviced, this device obtaining readouts of faults – even those unnoticed by the driver – and rectifing them.

L H injection assumes a key position. A heated wire (the air mass sensor) ensures the precise answer to the fuel quantity required at any moment, and this is delivered to the intake valve. A causal chain is then set up. Optimal combustion = higher energy utilisation = lower fuel consumption = lower pollutant emissions. Four petrol engines with power outputs of 170 kW, 210 kW, 240 kW and 300 kW in six, eight and twelve cylinder versions are available.

Boardroom in motion: the long and the short of it is the chauffeur's best friend, the stretched 600SEL. which follows in the best traditions of the Pullman-Limousine of a couple of decades ago. Its acquisition would relieve the corporate purse of at least £87,000, depending on what boardroom toys were specified

Shot against the spectacular Pembrokeshire coastline in South Wales, the sleek 300SL shows why it is the choice of Royalty and former Grand Prix drivers. The electrically-operated hood can be raised or lowered in a mere five seconds by means of no less than 58 sensors and computers, 89 electric motors and 1.4-miles of wiring loom

The basic level is represented by the six cylinder M104 series, already proven, but now increased to 3199 cm³ by enlarging bore and stroke.

The next level consists of two V8 engines of 4.2 and 5.0 litres, developing 210 and 240 kW. These are based on the M119 version and have hypereutectic aluminium alloy crankcases, with cylinder liners using electrochemically exposed silicon crystals.

It is 50 years since Mercedes-Benz used a 12 cylinder engine, (last seen in the W154 racing car), and the new one embodies real technical brilliance of a high order. The crankcase has the same features as the V8, but more attention has been given to minimizing noise by stiffening the crankcase, ribbing the cylinder heads, isolating the intake manifold from the engine by rubber elements, shrouding the injection nozzles and improving the geometry of the camshafts.

The new M120 V12 has an identical right hand cylinder head to that of the M104 six cylinder engine. The proven four valve technology – two inlet and two exhaust valves – exists in all engines. Valve timing is performed by overhead camshafts – two for the six, and four for the eight and twelve cylinder engine – driven by duplex roller chains. All valves have maintenance free bucket tappets.

Electrically controlled variable valve timing is probably the most important new feature of all these engines. The matching of sprocket wheel and camshaft is varied by means of a hydraulic actuator for each intake camshaft as a function of engine speed and torque by means of helical toothing, which produces a change in valve timing. The appropriate parameters are registered and the intake camshaft is controlled by the control unit of the electronic fuel injection system.

Design

It is Mercedes' policy to retain marked similarity in all models. It is fortunate therefore that the 1972 S was such a sound shape, the design being steadily refined to an art form over the past two decades.

The wind tunnel has assisted in this pursuit of the perfect design. This time, a more deliberate reduction of trimming has given strength to the symbolic force of the shape. The flush, and now double glazed, windows are at one with the flowing side contours, and the whole concept fits into the Mercedes-Benz marque identity.

The headlights are better, with variable focus reflectors and a four-lamp system, and although the windscreen is 8.6 per cent larger, the wipers now sweep 90 per cent instead of only 77 per cent of the glass.

The structural safety features, a Mercedes first, are capable of withstanding impacts from any direction. There is automatic seat belt height adjustment for front seats, together with air bags for both driver and front passenger, and three seat belts for the rear passengers.

Body quality, rigidity and durability, with high torsional and bending stiffness, has been achieved by using a multiplicity of machines in the factory designed to thoroughly test car shells, including electrodynamic shakers, followed by road testing on all surfaces at various proving tracks.

Mercedes-Benz 500E

The 500E differs from the 200E and 300E by being faster, lower and more brutal. It also has an abundance of power. The engine is electronically controlled with a databus system, and is restricted to 155 mph. Anti-roll bars and dampers give the car perfect balance.

The 500E is built at the Porsche works from specially made parts. Porsche were involved in the car's design, which explains its qualities. It was a good Mercedes to start with, but Porsche have turned it into a wonder car, minus the grand aura of the S class. It disassociates itself from beauty as well, spurning the two + two lunacy.

Above

Its 3-litre engine in 24-valve form will power the 300SL to 143 mph, and from 0-to-60 mph in 8.3-seconds. But with a svelte sports car like this, such matters are of little concern to the discerning owner. Given its head however, the 300SL remains poised and handling is sharp yet neutral at high speed

Right

The 300SL 24-valve is an impressive looking car, but although the intelligent seats (which remember your chosen position) and ample storage cubicles are welcome, the black dashboard is somewhat gloomy. The single column-mounted stalk is overloaded with switchgear

World Markets and Competition

Positive opportunities for post-war export opened up after the devaluation of the Deutschmark. Contact was first made with Switzerland and Sweden, then Belgium, Spain and South America. Five years after the war Mercedes-Benz was represented in 44 countries; by 1952 it was 79, this tally having risen to 143 by 1959, and today across the globe.

Post-war sales in the United States, which started in 1952 with Max Hoffman as distributor, improved in 1964 when the Studebaker-Packard group collapsed, and Daimler-Benz took over the entire sales network. The company sold 85,000 cars in 1985, which was 16 per cent of Mercedes' production for that year.

The 1960s were a period of expansion for the company, Mercedes first buying up the Friedrich Krupp empire, followed by Henschel and Hanomag. In 1985 they acquired the remaining 50 per cent shareholding of Munich Engine and Turbine Union (MTU). This was followed by the takeover of Dornier GmbH of Munich, who were primarily concerned with space, aeronautics, medicine and systems-engineering. These are new areas, but the basic vehicle market has also been enlarged. In 1981, for example, Daimler-Benz acquired Freightliner-USA.

The company is an international giant. In 172 countries across the world there are 5900 Mercedes-Benz sales and services centres, meaning that in any corner of the globe a customer can find help and spare parts.

Above
Mercedes' bread and butter car, the 190, introduced in 1982, and targeted at the young executive buyer. It brought quality motoring to a completely different market. Built on the W 201 platform with an advanced five link rear suspension set-up, it was originally powered by either 1.9-litre petrol or diesel engines, and a year later came the 2.2-litre 190D and 2.3-litre 190E, with fuel injection

Left
£56,000 buys you this serious piece of muscle, which if flexed, will go up to 155 mph and pass 60 mph from a standstill in 6.0 seconds. In those terms, 19 mpg seems a reasonable price to pay. It is a 500E, a fine all-rounder assembled and tuned for Mercedes by Porsche, and photographed here at Lullingstone Castle

Above

Underbonnet shot of the Cosworth-developed four-cylinder 16-valve 2.5-litre engine, which produces195 bhp at 6750 rpm, zinging this '190-on-steroids' along at speeds up to 156 mph, and cracking the 0-60mph hurdle in 7.1 seconds

Right

Possibly the nearest you can get to a boy-racer car in the Mercedes range is the 2.5/16 190E, which has excellent performance supported by a fine chassis. The particular shade of metallic maroon chosen by Mercedes certainly suits the car, and the air-dam, skirts and spoiler add an appropriate macho touch.

Mercedes police vehicles in Holland. There being no suitable national vehicle in the Netherlands, the authorities have done the next best thing and gone for high build quality and reliable engineering

Design and production

The design for all Mercedes-Benz vehicles takes place at Sindelfingen, where around 2500 people work in the areas of styling, basic development, data processing and design. The basis for the development of all new vehicles is the specification book. This is a collection of the ideas from all departments concerned.

From these basic specifications, sketches and clay models are made. Using CAD graphics, the designers then develop alternatives from which the final decision is made by the Board of Management on which design to adopt; this is based on the final 1:1 scale model, complete in all detail.

This model is then scanned by an electronically controlled measuring machine which provides digital data for tool making and construction. The development of the exterior and interior take place in parallel. A total of around 12,000 drawings using CAD and NC systems are made for one new vehicle. More than 450 design engineers are concerned with this work at Sindelfingen.

Data processing – Digital stored data of vehicle profiles, in numerically controlled production facilities, are made after computers have investigated the structure, using the FEM-finite element method. Since Mercedes are exported world wide, differences of temperature, as well as laws and regulations are considered.

Testing – Aerodynamic tests in wind tunnels and endurance tests for longevity of components terminate in crash tests which normally consume 130 vehicles annually, including trucks and vans. There are also tests for heat, frost, and humidity.

This Dutch cop seems happy enough with his 300TE emergency vehicle. With folded flat rear seats, load carrying capacity is prodigious

Production – Mercedes-Benz manufacture the press tools themselves, which make the parts from sheet steel with precision. The most important is the numerically controlled milling machine, with five axis milling features, for the three-dimensional machine surfaces.

AMG

The initials AMG are those of the founder, Hans Werner Aufrecht, his former associate Erhard Melcher, and Grossapach, Aufrecht's birthplace. The company began in 1967, initially operating its tuning business from an old mill in Burgstall, before moving to larger premises in 1976 and then to a purpose built unit at Affalterbach, where they are presently located.

AMG have always been solely concerned with the development of Mercedes cars, making improvements to engine power and torque, as well as the chassis and bodywork.

The company's reputation has been formulated in competition and the race track. In 1989, the AMG team had seven wins in the German Touring Car Championship, defeating the BMW M3s with their highly tuned Mercedes 190s, which took advantage of an 'evolutionary' version produced for production road use. All 500 'Evo IIs' were quickly snapped up at their unveiling at Geneva. The race version is built up from a bare shell, with a complex roll-cage being fitted to stiffen the frame and increase tortional rigidity.

The gutted interior saves weight, as does the use of carbon fibre and Kevlar

reinforced plastics for the bonnet, boot lid and tail fin. The fuel tank is replaced by a 110 litre racing tank, situated in the spare wheel well. The suspension is essentially unmodified.

Since 1991, AMG have had the resposibility for the development, preparation and maintenance of Mercedes-Benz competition projects. Also, all AMG products are now sold through the Mercedes worldwide dealer network.

The 190 was outstanding from its inception, but the AMG version, with its six cylinder engine developing 234 bhp, together with better handling, is as close to engineering perfection as a Mercedes can get.

The AMG range consists of five key models;

AMG   190E 3.2 – 172 kW–234 bhp 305Nm torque
AMG   200E 3.4
AMG   300TE 3.4 – 200 kW–272 bhp 330 Nm torque
AMG   300CE 3.4
AMG   500SL 6.0 – 275 kW–374 bhp 550 Nm torque

All Mercedes cars arrive at AMG with power steering and brakes, but this layout is soon modified. For example, to prevent vibrations effecting the engine, the power steering pump is driven by the propshaft, not the powerplant itself. The AMG cars use 225/45 R16 tyres on 7.5 inch AMG light alloy wheels. The chief development engineer at AMG is Werner Frowein, and the body designer is Claus Hieke.

Failed attempt by Dutch traffic police to customise the front of a perfectly innocent 190. That only the front panels are damaged is testimony to the integrity of Mercedes build quality

Above

Dutch courage. Faced with a police 190 squad car, the big question when wondering whether to make a run for it, is do they hot them up or not? British traffic police say not. But would they tell you anyway?

Right

The 5.0-litre turbocharged Sauber-Mercedes C9 which won the Le Mans 24-hours in 1989 at an average speed of 136.695 mph, driven by Jochen Mass, Manuel Reuter, and Stanley Dickens. These cars finished first, second and fifth, beating the works Porsche 962C and Jaguar XJR9 teams

Duchatelet

The Belgian coachbuilding firm of Duchatelet started in 1968 as a bodywork shop, but by 1980, the concept of top-level improvements to mainly Mercedes motor cars was established with the assembly of the first prototypes, which were presented at the Geneva Motorcar Exhibition in 1981.

In 1982 and 83, the Duchatelet interior decoration programme produced three variants of Carat accessories named Clarity, Diamond and Cullinan. Diamond options were for Rolls-Royce and Bentley only, whilst Clarity and Cullinan were available from 1984 for the larger Mercedes variants. During the same period, a distribution network was set up in Europe, the United States and the Far East.

1985 saw the creation of production divisions for stretched limousines, whilst in 1987 the Duchatelet Security Division was formed. This department designs and manufactures anti-kidnap and fully armoured modifications that provide protection against high-profile ballistic assaults.

The company entered a partnership with the University of Liege in 1990 on the advice of Mercedes, which allows Duchatelet to meet the their rigorous demands.

The Clarity conversion includes leather and Amaretta-lined dashboards and steering columns, an MB TEX centre console, HI-FI and VCR with audio tape unit, together with Zebrano or walnut mouldings on doors and dashboard accompanied by a matching gearshift knob. There is also a stainless steel telephone rest, and a foldaway writing table. The rear armrest is designed to house a telephone and a refrigerator is fitted as well.

It is the W140 diplomatic stretched limo, with improved suspension, that is perhaps the ultimate Duchatelet modification however. The chauffeur is sealed off, and the passenger interior is equipped for work with computers, a telephone and fax, the best radio/Hi–Fi sound equipment and CD player, with discs controlled from an arm rest console.

Above right
A technician at Duchatelet welds together a complex spaceframe for a special project

Right.
A variety of Mercedes saloons await transformation to a higher plane, as conversion and tuning work proceeds in Duchatelet's crowded workshops

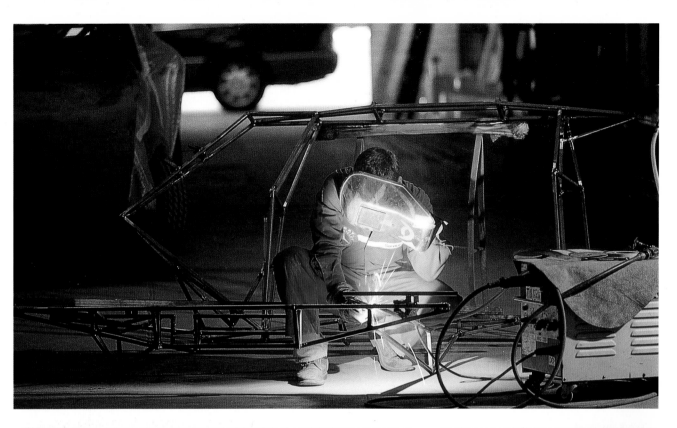

Right

Duchatelet operatives carefully preparing to install a special rear window. As if the average Mercedes wasn't sufficiently well-appointed, other modifications include more luxurious seating, lighting, and soundproofing, plus a whole array of stereo and video equipment

Below

The finished article: a 1991 S-class V12 600SEL. It is hard to understand why anyone would want to alter the standard machine, which at £68,000 is already very well appointed, its ride supple, its power output a thumping 408 bhp at 5200 rpm, and its top speed electronically governed to 156 mph